SIMPLY SCIENCE

Motion

by Melissa Stewart

Content Adviser: Mats Selen, Ph.D.,
Department of Physics, University of Illinois at Champaign-Urbana

Science Adviser: Terrence E. Young Jr., M.Ed., M.L.S.,
Jefferson Parish (La.) Public Schools

Reading Adviser: Dr. Linda D. Labbo,
Department of Reading Education, College of Education,
The University of Georgia

 COMPASS POINT BOOKS
Minneapolis, Minnesota

Compass Point Books
3109 West 50th Street, #115
Minneapolis, MN 55410

Visit Compass Point Books on the Internet at *www.compasspointbooks.com*
or e-mail your request to *custserv@compasspointbooks.com*

Photographs ©: Lester Lefkowitz/Corbis, cover; Creatas, 4; Bettmann/Corbis, 6; Mark E. Gibson/
The Image Finders, 7; DigitalVision, 8; Corbis, 10; Mark E. Gibson/Visuals Unlimited, 11, 15;
NASA, 12; PhotoDisc, 13; Gregg Otto/Visuals Unlimited, 16; H.Q. Stevens/Visuals Unlimited, 17;
Index Stock Imagery, 19; Cheryl A. Ertelt, 20; Unicorn Stock Photos/MacDonald, 21; Hal Beral/
Corbis, 23; Jack Ballard/Visuals Unlimited, 24; Larry Stepanowicz/Visuals Unlimited, 26; Eric
Hoffmann, 27; Ariel Skelley/Corbis, 28.

Editors: E. Russell Primm, Emily J. Dolbear, and Catherine Neitge
Photo Researchers: Svetlana Zhurkina and Marcie Spence
Photo Selector: Linda S. Koutris
Designer/Page Production: Bradfordesign, Inc./Erin Scott, SARIN creative

Library of Congress Cataloging-in-Publication Data
Stewart, Melissa.
  Motion / by Melissa Stewart.
      v. cm.— (Simply science)
Includes bibliographical references and index.
Contents: What is motion?—The first law of motion—Forces at work—The second law of
motion—The third law of motion—Machines and motion.
  ISBN 0-7565-0443-0 (hardcover)
  1. Motion—Juvenile literature. [1. Motion.] I. Title. II. Simply science (Minneapolis, Minn.)
  QC133.5 .S74 2003
  531'.11—dc21   2002010054

Table of Contents

What Is Motion? 5

The First Law of Motion 6

Forces at Work 10

The Second Law of Motion 17

The Third Law of Motion 21

Machines and Motion 25

Glossary 30

Did You Know? 30

Want to Know More? 31

Index 32

*Note: In this book, words that are defined in the glossary are in **bold** the first time they appear in the text.*

What is Motion?

Every time you throw a ball, you give it **motion**. The ball soars through the air and falls to the ground. It will roll for a while and then stop. It doesn't matter whether the ball is big or small. This is how a ball always acts when you throw it here on Earth.

If you could travel into deep space and throw a ball, it wouldn't act the same way. The ball would keep on moving in a straight line forever. It would never speed up. It would never slow down.

Throwing a ball gives it motion.

The First Law of Motion

Why does a ball act differently in space than it does on Earth? A scientist from England named Sir Isaac Newton was one of the first people to understand how objects move. In 1687, he wrote down three rules that explain the motion of objects, such as a ball. These rules are called laws.

Newton's first law of motion says that objects tend to keep on doing what they are doing. This law has two parts.

Sir Isaac Newton wrote the laws of motion.

This family will keep riding their bicycles in a straight line until they hit the brakes or turn the handlebars.

The first part says that if something is not moving, it will stay still unless some **force** acts on it. So if a napkin is resting on your kitchen table, it will stay there unless something makes it move. That something could be your hand or a gust of wind.

The second part of the law says that an object that is moving will keep on traveling in a straight line. It will move like this forever unless some force acts on it. A force can give an object motion. It can also stop motion or change the direction of something that is moving.

The objects on this table will not move unless some force acts on them, such as people passing them during dinner.

Forces at Work

Some of the most important forces are invisible. This means we cannot see them. We know they are at work because we see their results every day. The same force that makes a ball drop also causes apples to fall off trees. It is even what makes you land on the ground when you jump off a swing. This force is called **gravity**.

◀ We cannot see gravity, but it is the force that causes an apple to fall from a tree.

Gravity will also make this girl land on the ▶ ground when she gets off the swing.

All things make gravity, but only really big things like stars and planets make enough gravity so that we can easily notice it. Gravity pulls objects on or near Earth toward the center of our planet. It also pulls all the planets in our solar system toward the Sun. Without gravity, balls and cars and people would fly off into space. Without gravity, Earth and the other planets would not move in circles around

Earth's gravity pulls objects toward Earth. ▶

◀ *Without gravity, the planets would travel in a straight line instead of moving around the Sun.*

the Sun. They would move straight through the universe forever.

The force of gravity gets weaker as we move farther away from a planet or a star. Way out in space—far away from planets and stars—the force of gravity is very weak. If you could throw a ball out there, it would keep moving in a straight line for a very long time.

Another kind of force you feel every day is friction. This is a force that occurs when two objects are touching. Friction makes it hard for one object to slide over another object. If you slide a block across the

There is friction between the children's ▶
hands as they rub together.

floor, friction will slow it down until it stops. Friction between your shoes and the ground is the reason you can run around and play without falling down. Friction is also the force that makes heat when you rub your hands together on a chilly day.

faster and travel farther than it would if you had thrown it.

We use speed to measure a baseball's motion. Speed tells us how far the ball travels in a certain amount of time. Most big-league pitchers can throw a baseball at a speed of 95 miles (153 kilometers) per hour.

Isaac Newton also saw that if the same amount of force is applied to two objects, the heavier object is affected less than the lighter one. So if you throw a bowling ball and a baseball, the baseball will go faster.

The bowling ball is heavier than a baseball. If you throw it and a baseball with the same amount of force, the bowling ball will not travel as fast.

The Third Law of Motion

The last rule Isaac Newton wrote says that forces always come in pairs. The two forces are equal in strength, but they point in opposite directions. This means that if something is pushed forward, something else must be pushed backward. If you blow up a balloon and let go of it, air will rush out of the balloon in one

When the girls let go of these balloons, air will be pushed out of the balloons in one direction. This will cause the balloons to move in the opposite direction.

When the ball hits the wall, it exerts a force on the wall. The wall exerts an equal amount of force on the ball, which is what sends the ball back.

direction and the balloon will move in the opposite direction.

Sometimes it is not easy to see this law at work. When you throw a ball at a wall, you can see the ball bounce back to you. You cannot see the wall move, but it does move just a tiny bit. Because the wall is so much heavier than the ball, it does not move as much as the ball.

Pairs of forces can also be seen in nature. When a fish moves through water, it uses its fins to push the water toward its tail. The water pushes the fish forward. The amount of force on

A swimming fish shows that ▶
forces come in pairs.

the water is the same as the amount of force on the fish. The direction of the force on the water is opposite the direction of the force on the fish. This is how fish swim.

Machines and Motion

When you apply a force that starts, stops, or changes the direction of motion, your muscles do the work. For your muscles to do their job, they need **energy**. That energy comes from the food you eat.

If your muscles are not strong enough to do a job, a simple tool or machine can help you out. When a rock is too heavy to pick up, try rolling it up a ramp. If you have trouble breaking open a walnut or almond, try using a nutcracker.

Window fans, electric pencil sharp-

The boy needs energy to apply force to the peanut shells he is trying to open.

eners, and mixers are all machines. The electric motors in these machines use electrical energy to make the parts move. An electric motor is made of wire and **magnets**.

Magnets can make things move without touching them. You have probably seen magnets attract nails or paper clips. In an electric motor, the wire loops around the magnets.

When an electric **current** moves through the wire, the motor does its job. An electric current supplies the

This magnet attracts nails.

Some pencil sharpeners use electric motors, which are made from magnets.

force that makes a fan spin and a mixer mix. The motion of a fan cools the air. The motion of a mixer stirs up food. It is hard to imagine what the world would be like without motion.

A mixer depends on electric currents.

Glossary

current—a stream of electrical charges

energy—the ability to do work

force—something that starts motion, stops motion, or causes something to change its motion

gravity—a force that makes things on or near Earth fall toward the center of the planet

magnets—pieces of stone or metal that can make pieces of iron or steel move without touching them

motion—movement; a change in the position of something

Did You Know?

- You can hear because your ears can sense the motion of sound waves in the air. As the motion passes through your ears, messages travel to your brain. These messages carry information about how loud a noise is. They also tell your brain whether a sound is high pitched or low pitched.

Want to Know More?

At the Library

Laferty, Peter. *Force and Motion*. New York: DK Publishing, 2000.

Riley, Peter. *Forces and Movement*. Danbury, Conn.: Franklin Watts, 1999.

Tocci, Salvatore. *Experiments with Gravity*. Danbury, Conn.: Children's Press, 2002.

On the Web

Kids Corner—What is Energy?

http://clarkpud.apogee.net/kids/

To find out how to save energy and be safe around electricity

Pioneers in Energy

http://www.eia.doe.gov/kids/pioneers.html#Newton

To find out more about Sir Isaac Newton

Through the Mail

Adler Planetarium and Astronomy Museum

1300 S. Lake Shore Drive

Chicago, IL 60605-2403

To write for more information about how Newton's laws of motion affect the planets and their orbits

On the Road

National Air and Space Museum

Seventh and Independence Avenue, SW

Washington, DC 20560

202/357-2700

To learn more about how scientists and inventors have overcome the forces of gravity and friction to put people in space

Index

currents, 26, 29

Earth, 5, 6, 13–14

electric currents, 26, 29

electric motors, 26

electrical energy, 26

energy, 25, 26

fans, 25, 29

first law of motion, 6, 9

food, 25

force, 9

forces, 9, 10, 14, 21–23, 26, 29

friction, 14–15

gravity, 10, 13–14

machines, 25–26, 29

magnets, 26

measurement, 18

mixers, 26, 29

muscles, 25

Newton, Sir Isaac, 6, 17, 18, 21

nutcrackers, 25

pairs of forces, 21–23

pencil sharpeners, 25–26

planets, 13–14

ramps, 25

second law of motion, 17–18

solar system, 13

space, 5, 14

speed, 18

Sun, 14

third law of motion, 21–23

tools, 25

universe, 14

About the Author

Melissa Stewart earned a bachelor's degree in biology from Union College and a master's degree in science and environmental journalism from New York University. She has written more than thirty books for children and has contributed articles to a variety of magazines for adults and children. In her free time, Melissa enjoys hiking and canoeing near her home in Marlborough, Massachusetts.